More Courage Than Few

PoeticMoment

For Mara Ann,
the little girl whose birthdays were forgotten
who was found crying underneath beds
who checked herself into a
mental health center at 21
you did the best you could.

Contents

Foreword

I often hear writers say, producing a book feels like bringing a child into the world. It is a joyous occasion. This wasn't the case for me. Writing this book felt like carving out the death inside me. It felt like going places I never wanted to return to. Having to clean up my mess and others. It was the first time I gave myself permission to acknowledge my truth. To go back to the beginning. I had to accept that I didn't know which wound needed to be healed first. There were too many. Over 26 years of living I began to realize I hadn't processed any of my traumas. I was a walking time-bomb.

"More Courage Than Few" is a collection of poems as a result of grueling hours of therapy, and my conversations with God. They are the sickness, the abandonment, but also the hope. These poems are the story of every adult trying to rescue and love the child they once were. And there lies the beauty. That if you choose, turmoil does not have to be infinite. Help will come.

I hope you find pieces of yourself here. I hope you know that you are brave. You are more than what you've allowed yourself to believe. Life lies within you, it always has.

More Courage Than Few

<u>Things</u>

I am 26
I have survived some things

Like what? she asks.
I laugh,

Maybe I'm dramatic
Things could be worse

And things are? she asks.
I hesitate.

> [If I avoid the plural
> long enough, I can clean
> up the beginning before
> she notices]

I am 7
I have survived <u>something</u>

Do you want to kiss me? she asks.
I freeze,

> [I don't remember
> the rest]

I am 10
I have survived <u>two things</u>

Do you want to see him? she asks.
I nod,

> [I start a revolving
> door]

I am 13
I have survived three things

Does it hurt? he asks.
I lie,

> [I purge, ashamed
> to put anything else in my
> mouth]

I am 18
I have survived four things

How many attempts? they ask.
I forget,

> [I hope to be saved
> from interrogation]

I am 21
I have survived five things

Do you forgive me? she asks.
I tremble,

> [I lay on the
> ground, coddled by the
> abuser]

I am 26
I have survived some things

Like what? she asks.
I laugh,

Maybe I'm dramatic
Things could be worse

And things are? she asks.
I smile.

Where would you like for me to start?

<u>Seattle</u>

<u>Departure</u>

Flight leaves in an hour

I haven't left for LAX

Plane is boarding

I haven't made it through security

Flight takes off

I haven't heard from you

Seattle

Arrival

Whenever I am on a plane,
I'm reminded of times I tried to make you love me
Out the window I see the miles my heart never landed with yours

Connecting flight: cancelled

Stranded
No back up plan

I traveled for you
And now love and flying don't feel the same
My feet no longer leave the ground
I am unafraid of crashing

Burial
loading...

Overheard at church:
"*When you don't grieve,*
  you have all these funerals you haven't gone to yet."

Father is on the ofrenda;
Alive,
but to me;
Dead

At the funeral,
I will wear red

My hair pulled back
  His features on display
    They stare as I sit front row,
      I smirk inside

A bastard claiming a surname does not have clearance for sorrow

The whispers act as fans at my Spanish homecoming
My black face truth,
      a eulogy full of lies everyone should know

Reasons why I must bury him;
again

Only now,
I won't bring him back to life.

Family History

Family history tends to be important. It shows a derivative of origin and how certain things become more dominant in you in the years to come (i.e. body type, complexion, attitudes, behaviors are all said to be traced back to the DNA). In my family I was passed down a certain strain. Granny had battled with it in the 60's, before it had a name. Auntie wrestles around with it currently, and she can't get it tamed. Mama was put in a hospital once and still struggles; though she won't admit it's the same. And now I, the youngest in this generation, have it deep in my veins. Most black families have only one remedy for this beast, *Just pray about it baby, that's all you need.*   But I have watched this monster ruin lives right before me and prayer wasn't always the best defense. Neither were pills loaded with side effects, so I'd prefer to endure its nuisance. I guess I couldn't pray as strong as my elders and I know I am not as strong as my grandmother's shoulders. I am in the war of a lifetime with a score that is not in my favor.

Depression is winning.

The doctors say, that's what it wants you to think. That mental health is the toughest of enemies. It eats and feeds off how you feel and alters how you think. It is a gene that gets passed on from baby to baby, hand-me-down clothing for you to easily fit into. I haven't grown out of it yet. I haven't been able to win. Although every time it knocks me down, I still find the strength to get up again and again. It is sucking the life out of me. How my pupils dilate back into precious years I tried to take off my life. Depression comes inside. I never invite it over. It knew my family's history and picked me to carry out its legacy. Do you know how hard it is to find joy when happiness is the temporary disguise depression uses? I cannot rely on the Aztec and African strength flowing through me. So I must find new ways to fight back, in order to merely survive.

Conform to Confirm

On this rainy night I eat pizza with a stranger/
    a southern boy
His accent leaves dents in my cheeks
Stretching deep down his back
    a lush of never ending curls
My blushing frequently tags his laughter

                        Attraction?

He shares his bewilderment about life
Voice shaky, eyes nervous
Interviews me on ways of survival
Listens closely when I speak
Narrates his birth chart
    in hopes of matching with mine
He wants to know more about me

                        False alarm.

I know women who would love to be here
I am not them
Men are accessories
Earrings I have to remind myself I'm woman
They are not the jacket I find my gangster in
How I have to lighten my step for their convenience

                        Maybe.

Room 221 / seven

Nurses have told me the procedures would be painful, beyond the threshold of what average people can handle, nearing unbearable. Provide me doses of medication to ease the torture I will soon receive. They call it recovery, to lay down and let the body hurt while feeding it drugs. A numbing agent to prevent me from feeling anything at all. Sounds like prescribed depression. What they don't know is, I've been here before. Standing in front of doctors telling me what my body can and cannot withstand. Underestimating the strength of me, my blackness, and what it means to be anything other than normal. How this body is used to pain, most times from its own hands. I have pulled my insides out and watched as the blood dripped from my lips. Watercolors in a toilet bowl.   Burning my throat, in search of perfection. Explained the madness away. Refused nutrition to get a better look at my bones. How the stretch marks hold each other tighter when the skin droops. I've sat with the ugly in the mirror, only to scratch more scabs and digest more hate. More reasons to not love this sanctuary. The nurse thinks I am afraid of not waking up. As if there haven't been days where that was my final wish before bed. She does not know my only fear is to never heal. Never become like new. To be fortunate enough to know what loving my body feels like. Cutting me open is just a reminder of my own imprisonment. It's familiar —

At seven, most learning takes place through something called "concrete–play–type–experiences." Where a child uses their body or hands to manipulate things to gather meaning. For example, if a child wanted to understand texture, you would give them the freedom to feel different surfaces. The response is supposed to generate an accurate depiction of the world around them.

The first time my body held me captive was when it caved before it grew. It slumped when it should have been afraid. Poured, when it should have ran. Chose to play with a manipulator. I am told a physical reaction can also be deceptive. A child's brain cannot always decipher when boundaries have been crossed. Generating a natural response where humiliation swims. My therapist says it was a moment of physical affection I had been lacking, making it impossible to flee.   Doesn't make it less confusing. Two little girls level the playgrounds. My body, forced with hers to experience what I explored as closeness. Emotion hard to capture; though intimacy present. The roles started to blend, and when they did, the story lost its name and therefore its empathy. It tinted to unfortunate. Hatched into hard to explain. Leaving shame and guilt to become the childhood scars on my elbows. Mistakes I sometimes forget are there and reminded of when examined. When touched and seen naked in the light. A mention of something that was wrong but unsure why. A girl–hood secret to carry with me forever. Victim and circumstance have become synonyms. My body is an opponent that needs to be overcome. The one thing in this world I cannot trust because it still yearns. Offers itself up for dissection and never considers the violations that may fester.   Quick to chase the feeling of understanding first touch, while hiding from it all the same. I was asked if I wanted to play with attention and found   sexual submission. The foundation of my pain, confusion, and hostility. The monster in the mirror I'm forced to look at when the playing gets rough. Forced to acknowledge and fix. To rumble with in the grey.

Flooded Daisies

The silk, emerald field of daisies

— dipped in white and lemon —

obstructed with Persian blue

The pain is a treacherous flood I
drown in without notice

The mirage is soon absent and I return immersed

Thrusting to the top for breath, where flowers drift

Reminders of my futile hope

This ocean will eventually drain
and I will collapse to the surface;

enamored by the daisies again

It is routine

Tormented by the allure then having to relive the twisted

No /one / thing can be
entirely beautiful,

including me
I am learning this

How peace and chaos are equally yoked,

two sides of the same coin, and two
faces to the same body.

Wither

At 24, I tell myself I am in love with him. A lie always reveals a darker truth. He is my sacrificial lamb; responsible for trademarking this body. Man will always know something I don't. So I chose to lay raw with him for the first time to learn. With no piano playing and the fireworks dull, my insides began to wither. My heart began to break, and I imagine

> *What was God thinking?*
>
> *Why would He purposefully suffocate a cloud?*
>
> *Tell His daughter she can't come home?*

He moans, interrupting my thoughts to hand me back a lie in return. Looks deep into my eyes trying to see past the dark. Nothing inside of me is on, no matter how bad I wanted it to be. This is not the intimacy I prayed for. As if truth could surprise me in the end. It can't. It is forever the piece of furniture I ignore in this room.

Greenhaven

I fell in ~~love~~ with a girl whose wounds I found safe. Common to love the wicked and to feel understood in disorder. A reminder of home. Needing the needy. She was a thorn in arms clothing. Hands that appeared to stretch to ice my wounds. Never realizing she was adding to the infection. We found communion in one another's blood. Each gash out bleeding the other's. Each insecurity over pouring until there was nothing good left. There was nothing good about us. A collision of unchecked traumas. Where pins and needles is how we chose to feel. *Toxic.*   *Controlling.*   *Jealous.* Everything that reminded us of them. The examples we were given on relationships. The mothers we swore we would try to be better than. Where unions came with frequent turbulence. And the only way to win is by having control over the other. We made promises to be better, but it's all we were ever exposed to. I never feared another human being before you.   A lesson in forgiving unintentional evil. To unwrap love and find codependency underneath. Took years to break myself free. And what was left was a shell of a woman. Knowing how love shouldn't feel, but too weak to ask for anything more.

Choice Of None - More Courage Than A Few

*The devil can have
me if God does not
want me, because
what would be the
point of living?*

am not brave. My words have not yet matured. They are drops resting on the roof of my mouth. And I am trying to protect them as long as I can before they go unhinged. Become children who have no respect for their mother. Rash and harsh, honesty held captive for too long. So for now, it's better for the both of us if I choose silence. Allow your ignorance to lather every color in this room with coal, while I assert resistance. While I stand in this truth, and no amount of blood could move me and make me run. Abandon it, the way you're about to do to me. So you'll talk, and I'll pretend to listen. Juggle the different ways I could tell you you're wrong. Find distractions to preserve my peace. Weep in silence knowing a resolution is beyond us. Remind God of His promise to me. Understand the wolves are ready, and I am being tossed at their feet.

<u>Side A</u>
Overheard: *She doesn't mean anything to anybody but herself*

It's 8:30PM

     I'm getting life advice from The Proud Family
     I sit in bed removing my acrylics
     Avoiding the time
     You're on your way over soon
     Said you'd leave within the hour
     I have thirty minutes to go
     It's LA
     You'll probably be here by ten
     I have work in the morning
     This reminds me of a SZA song
     Can't remember which one
     I just know she sang about heartbreak
     and dealing with people who make you late for work

It's 8:32PM

     I am curious if your thought process is as jumbled as mine
     Why do I always agree to wait on other people?
     This reminds me of my father
     I don't care about the pending conversation
     You are already better than him if you show up
     Please show up

It's 8:34PM

     My eyes keep catching the clock in increments of two
     As if the universe is setting the stage,
     for the both of us.

<u>Side B</u>

Tonight

    I rush home for you
        Despite assuming you've lost the address
        Knowing my rushing would dim to waiting
        Still, I drive 89 miles per hour
        Trying to beat GPS's projection
        I do
I enter these walls in a panic
        The flame in the candle still burns
        I hurry to tidy up
        Hoping in the chores you'd distract me
          With an "otw" text,
                      call,
                              or knock on the door
        I receive none
I turn on the heat
        Trying to trick my mind into believing I am enough
        in my own home
I sit
        Put my bonnet on,
        surrender to the gloom of your ghost
        You always prove me desperate
I light the blunt
        Inhale your inconsistency
        Watched the shadows of your habits imprint my walls
I head to sleep
        But not before the candle fades

Palms

In the front of my childhood home are palms. Magnificent trees that stand taller than the 2-story house my mother managed to afford. I once heard her say she wanted everyone to stop and stare when you turned down our block. She needed something that signified shelter. A war cry for how forgotten she was made to feel as a little girl. This south central single mother was a long way from home. There wasn't much she could take besides the allusion of protection, leading me to fall in love with them. They became the reference for the good times. When I was outdoors more than in.   Where bikes with empty soda cans transformed into motorcycles. And the basketball nets wilted. The sun would beam so hard, my skin dried like raisins. Tangled and knotted hair was evidence of wild adventure. The laughter was real. Ice cream trucks blared a tune of no worries. When I ran until my lungs made like hot coals in my chest, and the only clock I acknowledged were palm leaves darkening. Palm trees were my atlas, and the place that I found you near. In the same place my mother hurried away from, yards of gravel with fountains of palms paved an aisle of safety. And there you lie, resting peacefully *next* to them. That should have been a clue. You living on the outside of memory's hug. Never finding me in the middle. Forcing yourself to observe love, never actually becoming part of it. Keeping me at bay. Just close enough to claim and watch. The palms are polluted now because of you. They are not the keepsake I can take with me years from now. They do not cast shade and signal me back home. They repeat the same empty version of love my mother never wanted me to know.

Las rosas estan muertas

~~Friday night~~

I lay in a king–size bed full of skeletons
Hopeful the dead will burrow inside me
I've heard it's easiest this way

So I could use:
    a lifeless body,
    momentary satisfaction,
    and nothing to hope for

I've tried:
    living without love,
    breathing without living,
    and feeling without giving

All of which have become dead roses on my mantle
Decorations for the departed
Reminders
    of how I need to water my loneliness with more
    than thirst

I am not artificial
I know this heart needs more than warmth to survive
But tonight; the frigid will do

Behold

I'm called many names I shouldn't
answer to, because I am not what I
appear to be. This body is deceiving
despite its existence. It enters the
room before my purpose cries. Domi-
nates the conversation, though I am
overcome with distrust. Paranoid of
anyone who comes near. How could
you already want a woman you
haven't learned? Whose pain you
haven't understood? And trauma you
haven't held? My value is visible, not
abstract. Something to be won. What
a sick reality to observe. My carcass
thriving despite my soul's loathing.

Warn the people
Tell them not to be fooled
Tell them I am not well
This body is a cloak for decay

<u>1992</u>

When I was born, I did not cry after my mother gave birth. This was my first experiment with lying. They say infants cry when they come out of the womb because the change in environment can be overwhelming. They say the ordeal that is birth can also be physically taxing. Both of which were true, and yet   silence. An audience who didn't ask questions. A mother who was thankful I wouldn't grow to be a man. A father who had a wife to go home to. And a baby left to two children, taken into arms and labeled untroubled. God forbid they saw me crying. To adhere to their mess instead of living with my own. What a perfect place to learn how to distort the truth and make myself convenient for others. A story that's easier to swallow. Imagination and reality will melt into one another because I am mute. Questions will go unanswered and I learn just how easy it is to exist, and be a secret. I shocked everyone in the room with my stillness. Bathing in toxins should not produce peace. But acceptance and approval was my intention. I learned how to make lies digestible without using my tongue. Enough truth for make-believe to look real. Dazzle you with fake charm so you feel comfortable and I don't feel ashamed of being. A way to take control of the narrative I never had a hand in. Rewrite my own story, and never give someone else the satisfaction to define my truth.

Therapy For Black Girls

To older black women, therapy is a luxury that should never be afforded. Because who has time or money to waste talking about my problems, when the world is full of problems, except people who like to create problems? Me going to therapy is a problem according to my mother. A debt   rather than an investment. A 30-day trial to take, not a lifelong commitment. Something that can be worked out through God, not a human. Because an hour can't change you, let alone be the answer to the way things are. My mother says, how could you harp on the bad instead of revel in the good? There ain't no room for me to be broken around glass. No room to say how I feel when the wounded mother is deafening. When she knows best, because she's been here before me. How she presses forward without acknowledgment & labels it strength. Causing me to carve out time just to backtrack the loss. Of her, of him, of everything stolen & this is my time to file the paperwork. Reach out for help in hopes of getting everything back. To talk life through to someone who is willing to look in the wreckage with me.

Ironic, my therapist is still an older black woman. That despite the opposite sides we stand on, she will still know & see me better than anyone else in this world. Or at least she's supposed to. Like you. At least pieces of my story will dissolve into her lineage & we'll become sistren. Two women trying to work past the confusion with dialogue & patience. Myths we were told society would have with us. With us, it will always be the child & the parent. A battle for who gets to sit in whose seat. & there are some mornings when the daughters cannot parent the mothers. When we need a day to weep in silence for the youth we never got to play with. Tears for the mom who hasn't quite got it yet. For the love that sometimes hurts to give. A room where it's okay to cry. To say life isn't fair without judgement. To cradle the little girl inside & tell her I love you, I understand you, & none of this is your fault. For that, I'd be glad to be called privileged. To be spoiled. If loving myself enough to do the work is having it easy, then I know some mothers who are burdened. Where the ratio of basic human needs met is how they measure their success. When their unresolved trauma gets compared to yours, and being better than their parents is all they reached for. So how dare we fix our noses up to complain. I refuse. For my future daughter, I refuse to be another by-stander when the questions get tough, & the truth gets sticky. I will admit I know nothing but still learning, still trying to go past the best I know how to do. I'm in therapy for her mommy, not because of you.

woman : woman

Your girlfriend finds her way to my doorstep in search of answers I assumed she already had.

> *It's embarrassing to show*
> *all your cards that way.*

I wish I felt remorse. I am a victim too I presume. I fell into your traps of thrill and believed the sweet nothings uttered. I took your word as truth. Dismissed intuition. I wonder for a moment

> *How does it feel?*
> *To be on the outside looking in?*
> *To see the picture behind the fog; a*
> *smeared reality?*

She's late. Behind the curve of what everyone else already knows. We all know, discussed, met, and there she stands blindly. She does not know who you really are anymore, but I did for a moment. And the only way she can gather herself is by collecting the pieces of you she thinks I have. I have nothing of yours. That was intentional. Closure cannot be found in a place that has moved on.

honey dutch _____

Girl meets lighter and never looks back. Found a way to command noise to be still. To be aware without paranoia's touch. Anxiety finally cried itself to sleep. And the rain outside pours. She creeps into the jungle, just to hear the sounds of everything but herself.
A quiet night, where a throne awaits.

To be high is to savor nature after surviving solitary confinement. To unlock a part of your mind while muting another. It's freedom. Where life has rhythm. A never ending beat that changes with your chosen mood. A sway. Your body and spirit dance and you do not fear the world's scrutiny. You no longer carry the unforgiven. The sleep becomes rest and the food turns into feast. A check-in with survival. To adhere to living and feeling more than your pain. Saying for now, we tell the God of death another time.
I have a flight I need to catch.

*smoke before you read

breakdown #26387

I wrapped myself in a prayer cloth
                  and fell to the floor in agony

    Surely God must hear this cry,
    He must feel this pain

It was the only thing I knew to do —
Call out to the one responsible for this life

This was not a moment of blame, but of devotion
Fully taking my hands off the wheel while heading over a ledge;

Faith is what they call it:
To be on the verge of death but know you'll survive

The screams stop
The tears dry
The pain recedes; if only just a bit.

Aguilera

The nurse tells me,

"You don't look like your last name"

           my teeth clench

My father's from Chihuahua

The only time I claim him
is when I have to reclaim me

A thief,

         even in absence

Chaka Khan Was A Slur

I would always get frustrated when it came time for others to do my hair. I would invest hours between my mother's legs to appear docile to the masses. The circus of burnt wooden spoons covering ears and broken glass tables. How the rollers would engrave circles into my neck. In turn, my hair is a task I never learned how to do. In private, my mother would tell me I had too much, a signal of being blessed. In public, she said it was wild / thick / and hard to control. A metaphor for the black woman I grew into. Chaka Khan was my given nickname from my sister back then. A woman I resented. The audacity she had to let her hair just be. The glory she found in its thick-ness, the fullness of her lips, and the way she commanded a room using only her voice and hair. How strong it must have been to be all natural without shame. To carry a crowd and never have your blackness critiqued or studied. I was not every woman. I fell into the trap of perms and relaxers to tame this growing mane, mama said anything to make it manageable. At times, I still straighten myself out and make my blackness easier to handle. Fell into the background because I was tender head-ed and not mature enough to receive this comparison. Refused combs and brushes in protest. Childlike choices developed into adult actions making me still hard-headed to this day. Leaving me to learn the work of a beautician from scratch, how to love the native and oil the damaged roots.

<u>(323)-369-xxxx</u>

terrible how

you and I

have nothing

ironic

me not

broke

but whole

<u>"I'm out"</u>

A final goodbye to love feels like mourning the dead. Something I've never been good with. I hate funerals. Hate looking at the body before the burial. Hate the sound of crying. Hate being asked to speak. Hate my hand being held. Hate the aesthetic. The "sorry for your loss" that comes in different dialects. My body prefers to not be active, just in the room. Paying respect.

The same goes for you. And how I have to close this chapter of us for good. The back and forth, the ride, the adrenaline. All the ways my body felt while you attempted to love me. And now I have to acknowledge I am walking away with nothing. Years of a gamble, only to end in a casualty. Memories are not keep-sakes. And that reality deserves numbing grief. It deserves time to hurt, but only for a service. To make a decision that I cannot come back from, by choosing me and mummifying the past. Something I will never want to unwrap again.

Moving ahead knowing all what if boxes have been checked. No other outcome was destined to lead us here. Where we end. Where goodbye is hiding under our breaths. And there's nothing else we can do because the fire is catastrophic. With little left to want to rescue if anything at all. So the adíos is bitter, it's blunt. It tastes like tequila on a summer's day. A kiss between the fin-gers for having the audacity to let me leave. Let me pick out the flowers. The casket. What you wear on your final day.

My last moment to display just how invested I really was. How deep my love ran. It is a time to rejoice, because your season has ended. The weight is off my back and the angels have called you home. Becoming just another picture in a scrapbook for my grandkids to inquire about···

And when they ask, I will smile. Rub the date and think back to my time with you and I will be thankful for the times with me. When I chose something greater than not being alone. Believing unnecessary stress was knitted to love. Thank God for the dead. They are reminders you have the choice to keep living. To make arrangements on how to move forward knowing forward is the direction you're going. Have the pastor say his final words, tell the pallbearers to come, and let the choir sing.

Not Today

I told my therapist I didn't feel like unpacking my trauma today
I'd rather leave it on the floor and hang it up next week

She smiled
Said,

>*There she is*
>*I love when you talk to me like that*
>*Just living in your authenticity*

Honesty isn't always comfortable,
It can be blunt
It can be sharp
It can divide a room
And that is okay

Me using this voice when it matters is okay
Me saying, *not today*
is okay.

Wedding Photos

In my dreams, the wedding pictures are somewhat empty. My spouse is always a Gumpy outline in white chalk. A silhouette that wraps itself near me perfectly. A space that has been removed; I assume due to someone messing with time travel. And then there is me, standing next to the vacancy overjoyed. Unbothered that the love of my life is a frame. This is the part of the poem where you start to consider the metaphor. There is none. This is just an observation. Of understanding sexuality and how little I actually know about it. Fluid I believe is the term. A substance that has no fixed shape and yields easily to external pressure. The pressure of being happy with whoever one decides. A woman. A man. Depends on the dream. Do all of God's gay children receive the same prophecy? A vision of how to contort love. To bypass ordinary and see tradition as binary. To rebel within the confounds of union. To be so sure of self by means of faith in the unknown. The ending we can't explain but know we deserve. Shown answers before the test on seeing someone's spirit, not body. I've never lusted after the bodies in the blueprints of my childhood dreams. Only loved beyond the first draft of possibility, and made room for other interpretations. I made room for other interpretations of my wedding day before I knew I wasn't allowed. Played with the idea of roles and where my heart may fall. Held tight to the firefly inside when found. Unapologetic about who I choose to love in my dreams but afraid of the nightmare when I wake up.

Gutsy women travel

My tour guide inquires about my traveling alone
I tell her once a month I decided to explore a corner of the earth,
    A place I haven't touched yet;
        To recover hidden features within me
There's a story there, she says
She reminds me
    I'm *woman*

        young

            brave
Words heavy enough to save lives
Tells me not to undervalue this experience
Encourages me to tell this story
No matter how it ends
Someone somewhere needs to hear it, she says

The tour ends
We embrace
I am leaving a piece of me here
It's in good hands

        ~ for Jen

handheld

she's still apart of you..

is she?

Father texts me   *your grandmother is dying.* The cancer in her 95 year old body has come to feast. And her hands aren't as brawny as they once were. She cannot fix a meal but has found peace in being the offering. To lie down and not fight the devil back.

Father didn't text me when my day of life came, *a n d   w e n t .* Another year of failing to acknowledge his tithe to the world. To not water the plant that's still living. He wants to wring me of emotion now. Twist salty oceans out of my flesh, hopeful I will baptize in amnesia or compromise. The stone in front of my heart cannot be moved by a scared boys hands.

My tears are not for the woman I do not know, but for the grip I should have had. The Spanish I should have learned. The tomatillos I could've peeled. The quiñce that wasn't celebrated. The family I'm a stranger to. I cannot bring myself to weep for deliberate distance. And I will not allow blood to wash over self-preservation.

virgo sun & scorpio moon

That little girl trauma can't live here no more
Mommy's baggage aint yours
Father's choices said nothing about you
God's creation isn't a mistake
Though that's what the cards said
You are more than the demons that keep you up at night
You are love, in its most beautiful form
The world just wasn't ready to receive you
You weren't ready to receive you
But we prayed it through
Still unsure of what lies ahead
Thank God you're willing to hold forgiveness
For patience is starting to move
There you are,
the rust is starting to give
I see the little girl you once were
She smiles,
knows healing is on the way
And we can't stop
Can't get tired when the work overwhelms
Because where there's hope,
there's life.

MacBook

*I have a secret
though I can't share it*

*My mind failed to expose
or give it life*

I know my intentions this go around

*So the bags are packed,
I am dressed,
and the blunt is being smoked*

This is the first time I am leaving you behind

*Locking the door to
good decision making,
reflection*

*I call this,
evolving*

*Making a wrong turn
and being ready
to collide*

*I will not be naive,
or appeal to the fantasy of others*

*I will demand what I want,
stand in the clarity of my voice,
and love every moment of it*

Down

My body fell 13,000 feet from the sky — it was the first time I remembered to breathe and wail a scream that released every fear I had allowed myself to take on. To look at the ground and demand it catch me in its hands carefully. Tell the clouds to make room, for this bird is finally learning to fly. Trust God more than ever before. My bucket list is dwindling. Who would have thought you could start living so young? That panic is just a manifestation of what you're unsure of. That real growth is knowing you can only focus on your part. So play it well, and don't be afraid to leap. The world will rejoice when you do. The blessings will pour into you, when you remember that looking down at the mountains you've climbed, is just as important as looking up.

Field of Dreams

Choosing me ain't been easy. It feels like putting puzzle pieces where they don't belong. The hard thing to do. Confusing. The thing that doesn't quite make sense. Making a different decision than you've ever made before. Taking care of yourself when you were never taught how. I'm a child using tools for the first time, with frequent errors and questions. *Was I really this empty? Did this vase only have purpose when stuffed?*

Only cleaned when the flowers died within me? God has been trying to get me alone. Something about Him doing His best work in isolation. He knows I hate my own company. I picked from an assortment of distractions to numb feeling hollow inside. Making it so that I was never really alone. I'd become irrelevant to myself. Waited to be told what I needed and deserved. Chose to be in a field rather than with my own soul. Seeped into others and ignored my original purpose. A constant echo of circumstances killing potential. And now; with the flowers gone, there is no one to shield me from me. The stadium hushes to hear what I have to say or think. And sometimes the thoughts are louder than my own voice. They scatter when the lights come on. Sometimes this body feels much bigger than it once did. My brain is heavy ceramic blocking my heart. Beginning a battle of man versus self that needed to be resolved. A meeting of good and evil who chooses to heal rather than ignore. That work can't be done in a garden. I can't get lost in the presentation. I must live in my reflection. To get lighter, but know that means you must be more careful when you carry me. Because I understand being alone and lonely are not perfect pairs. You can be stable without using others to hold you up. Life alone cannot be avoided forever. And I will swim in the journey of my own existence to experience it. If only to bloom.

"guess what mommy said?"

Mommy speaks on the sins of my father & the lessons she
wished she learned from her mother, in hopes of connecting with
her youngest daughter, & it's working. How she's laid down her
judgement to look at the painting from a different angle.
Said she had to ask herself what the real issue is.
What does she really want for me?

First mommy says,
    She does not want me to end up with a broke(n) woman
This is the first time me being groomed a caretaker
    was acknowledged
That in my 27 years I've saved enough people
It was time for someone to love me enough that I could rest

You are not the fruit at the bottom of the tree
Demand people reach for you
Avoid falling for beggars with open arms

Mommy says God will either give you what you want
    or change how you view it
That both roads lead to a victory
How relationships are not mistakes,
    but lessons
A parting gift if you & your partner must end

Mommy says suspicion is never random
Move with your spirit but know eventually you must let it go
& though the error may be the same,
    you've corrected it faster,
    thank God for growth

Life, is a journey with no final level to unlock
Being perfect all the time is simply a myth

Mommy says I deserve a king
& however that looks is alright with her

She felt the need to tell me her spirit is being washed
    Renewed
Her faults are shapeshifting,
    turning into things in common between two women
Genuine advice dressed in affirmation & wisdom
A step closer to understanding all of me

By admitting that I gave her permission to think
To question what really matters
& what matters will always be getting the very best
because I deserve it
& because I am worth it

I did better than I thought I would

A compliment to myself. The new self-talk. Look at what you've done my child, with the mess you were given. Found yourself in the mirror and named her beauty. Honored the disaster boldly. How you taught yourself to pray. To grab God by the ears and ask questions. Always listening for His voice. To thirst for more while following only your heart. To retain as much as you can. How you learned what was hot and cold on your own. Played with pain and talked with bliss. Chose to drown before you swam. To eat and be full again, after years of being empty. To forgive while hurt. To feel like no one has ever felt before. To show up, every — single — day. To have something to leave behind.

You've done alright.

<u>Joy</u>

The poems have left her for a bit

I was warned this would happen

*How a writer becomes silent
the minute they touch joy*

She's grazed joy by the hem

*Ran her fingers through its lace
as it passed by*

*Savored its edges,
melted into its intricate design*

Joy is big, swift, and full of grace

Is this is why her poems stop?

*No room for emotions
that weigh like quicksand?*

*My small voice can't be
heard over a forgiving heart*

This woman I'm becoming is so care free

These smiles are honest

The laughter is true

The quiet is marble

Joy radiates off me as I walk and the people notice

Call it a natural glow

They gather at my feet wondering what secret I have learned

I've learned no more than loving myself and living long enough to tell how

Patient on the days where I make mistakes

Fulfilled on days of just living

Acknowledgements

To my mother and my sister, I thank you both so very much for your patience with me over the years. You two were the first people I've ever loved and your love is the only reason I am still alive today. Our trio-tribe and how the three of us have survived over the years is why this book was even possible.

To my daddy, there are no words. It is because of you that I even know what a man's love should feel like. Thank you for stepping up and calling me yours. You are proof of how beautiful black men can be. You gave me room to learn where I came from and never once made me feel like I was anything other than your daughter.

To Edwin; my editor and angel, I could not have done this without you. Thank you for pushing me. For the long hours of editing and pulling the truth out of me even when I was afraid of it. At times I know this process was exhausting, but your faith in me and my story is what helped my healing. I thank God for you. This project was more than poetry, this was my life, and you made me feel fearless enough to share it.

To my poetry family; T–Rex, Cubano, & Mama Lyesha, I love yall more than words will ever express. I used this time to study your willingness to be honest to the page, and also your ability to love the process. Thank you, so much for loving all of me.

To my students; past / present / and future, I wrote this for you. This is for all the stories I've heard and all the lives I take home with me every night. You have been my biggest teacher during this process. You have kept me truthful and obedient. You constantly remind me just how important a child's voice is. It was through you, that I gave the child I was, the voice she deserved.

About The Author

PoeticMoment is an author, poet, educator, and community outreach organizer based in Los Angeles, California. She has been featured in numerous venues around the metropolitan area including Fly Poet, Da Poetry Lounge, EPIC, and SoFar Sounds.

As a spoken word artist, she has been nationally recognized at The National Poetry Slam, Long Beach Poetry Slam, Southern Fried Poetry Slam, and many more.

As a professor, she actively works within Education by helping to develop the next generation of incoming teachers. Her passion for understanding and navigating mental health and childhood trauma has led her to work with various organizations to raise awareness. Some of these organizations include BESE: State of the Mind Series, Step Up: Inspiring Women to Inspire Girls, and Radical Self Care Now! Her life's work is to use poetry as a means of communicating previously endured trauma and the hope the lies ahead.